Franz Wohlfahrt
Op. 45

Sixty Studies for the Violin

Complete

Books I and II

Edited by
Gaston Blay

ALLEGRO
EDITIONS

Franz Wohlfahrt (born April 7, 1833; died March 14, 1884) was a German violin teacher and composer who studied under Ferdinand David. He is most recognized for creating a basic training for violinists, especially with the etudes collected in his *60 Studies for Violin*, opus 45, in two volumes. The first volume is the first position only; the second moves through the positions. Wohlfahrt reportedly developed the etudes to provide what was then lacking in the study of the violin: a method for training young violinists developing both artistically and physically. In Wohlfahrt's time, it was common for musicians to take artistic liberties with scores in seeking to bring the composition to life, and this was perhaps especially true of his etudes, where he may have purposely left room for the violinist to explore the nuances inherent in their structural and harmonic development.

Published by Allegro Editions

Sixty Studies for the Violin (Op. 45, Books I and II)
ISBN: 978-1-64837-144-8 (casebound)
978-1-64837-143-1 PB (paperback)

Cover design by Kaitlyn Whitaker

Cover images: "Music Sheet" by danielo courtesy of Shutterstock;
"Violin front view isolated on white" by AGCuesta courtesy of Shutterstock

CONTENTS

BOOK I

No. 1 Allegro moderato 7
No. 2 Allegro moderato 8
No. 3 Moderato 8
No. 4 Allegretto 9
No. 5 Moderato 9
No. 6 Moderato 10
No. 7 Allegro moderato 10
No. 8 Largo 11
No. 9 Allegretto 11
No. 10 Moderato 12
No. 11 Moderato 12
No. 12 Allegro 13
No. 13 Moderato 14
No. 14 Allegro non tanto 14
No. 15 Allegro 15
No. 16 Moderato 16
No. 17 Moderato assai 16
No. 18 Allegro 17
No. 19 Moderato 18
No. 20 Allegro 19
No. 21 Allegro 20
No. 22 Allegro 21
No. 23 Moderato 22
No. 24 Moderato assai 23
No. 25 Allegro 23
No. 26 Allegro 24
No. 27 Allegro 24
No. 28 Allegretto 25
No. 29 Moderato 26
No. 30 Allegro 27

BOOK II

No. 31 Moderato 30
No. 32 Allegro 31
No. 33 Allegro moderato 32
No. 34 Allegro 33
No. 35 Allegro 34
No. 36 Moderato 35
No. 37 Moderato 35
No. 38 Moderato 36
No. 39 Moderato 37
No. 40 Allegro scherzando 38
No. 41 Allegro moderato 39
No. 42 Andante 40
No. 43 Moderato 40
No. 44 Tempo di marcia 42
No. 45 Moderato 43
No. 46 Allegro 44
No. 47 Andante cantabile 45
No. 48 Allegretto 46
No. 49 Allegro 46
No. 50 Allegro 48
No. 51 Moderato 49
No. 52 Andante 50
No. 53 Andante 50
No. 54 Allegro 51
No. 55 Allegro 52
No. 56 Andante 53
No. 57 Moderato assai 54
No. 58 Andante 54
No. 59 Moderato assai 55
No. 60 Allegro con fuoco 56

Franz Wohlfahrt
Op. 45

Sixty Studies for the Violin

Book I

Studies

⊓ Down - bow.
∨ Up - bow.

Hold the fingers down as long as possible. The left wrist plays lightly.

Franz Wohlfahrt. Op. 45, Book I.

Nº 1. Allegro moderato.

In the second, third and seventh Études the same bowings that were given for the first Étude are to be used.

№ 2. Allegro moderato.

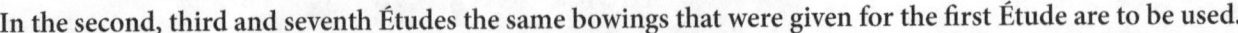

№ 3. Moderato.

Pay attention to G♯ on the D-string and to D on the A-string.
Look out for D on the A-string and for A♭ on the E-string

In the last three measures, employ the same bowing without change.

Nº 19. Moderato.

No. 20. Allegro.

№ 21. Allegro.

№ 23. Moderato.

No. 29. Moderato.

Franz Wohlfahrt
Op. 45

Sixty Studies for the Violin

Book II

No. 36. Moderato.

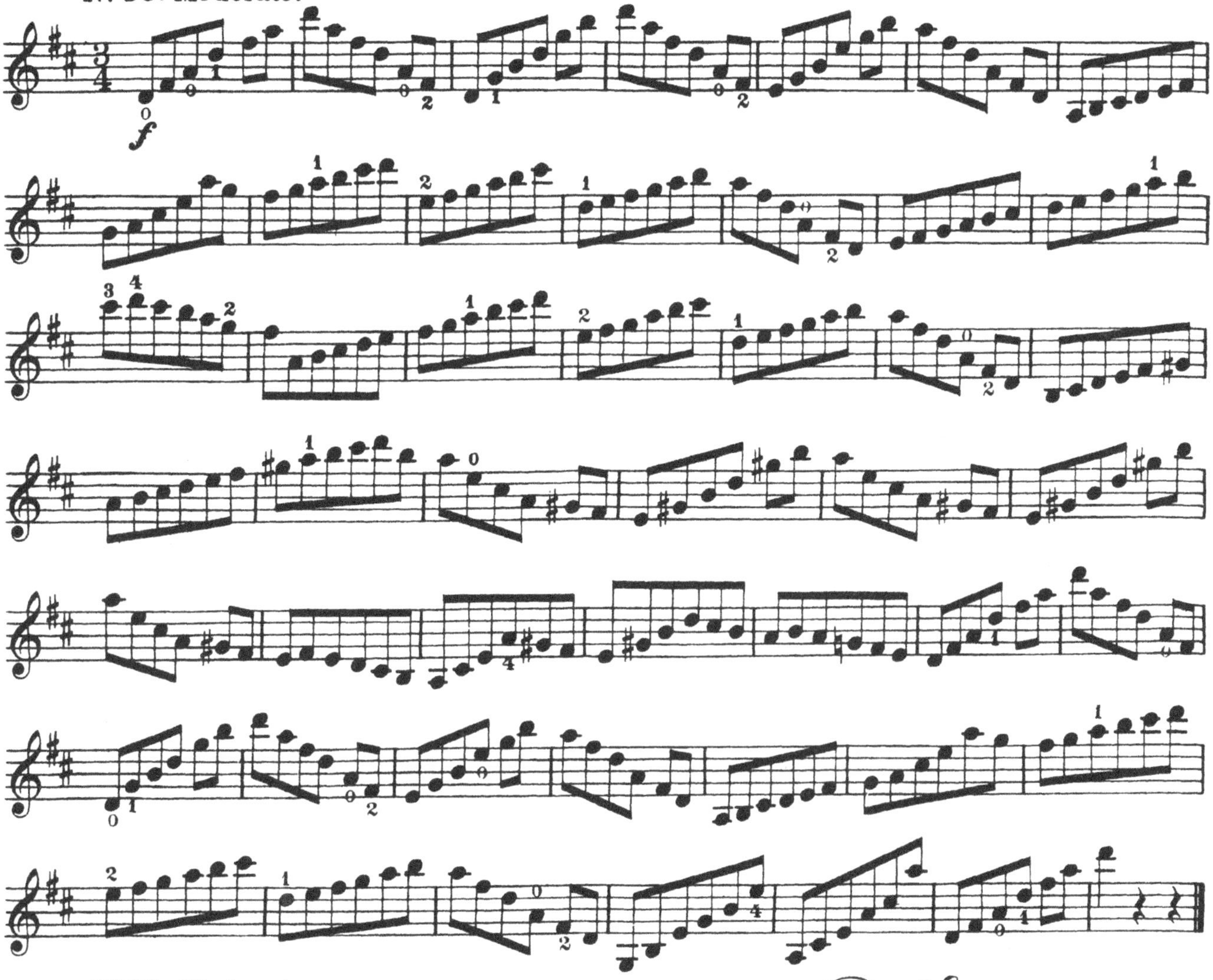

No. 37. Moderato.

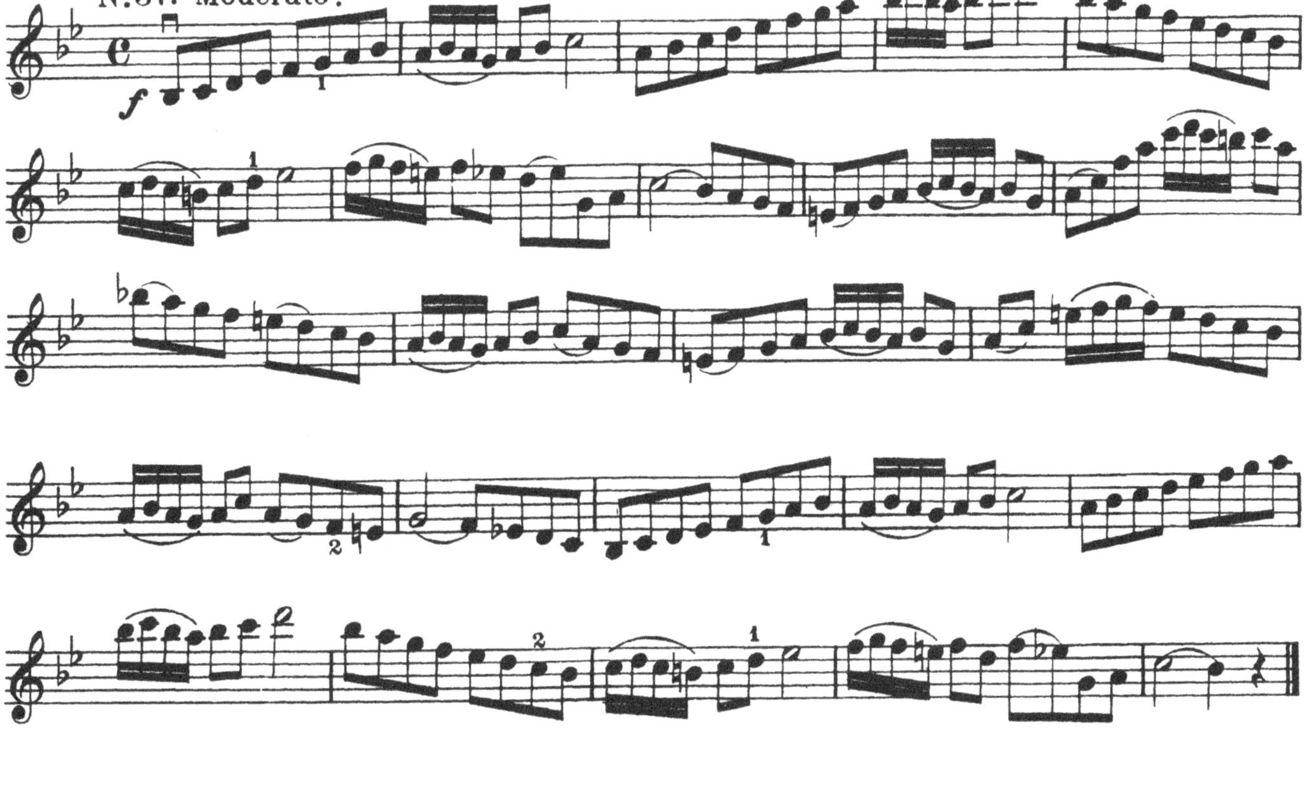

№ 38. Moderato.

No. 39. Moderato.

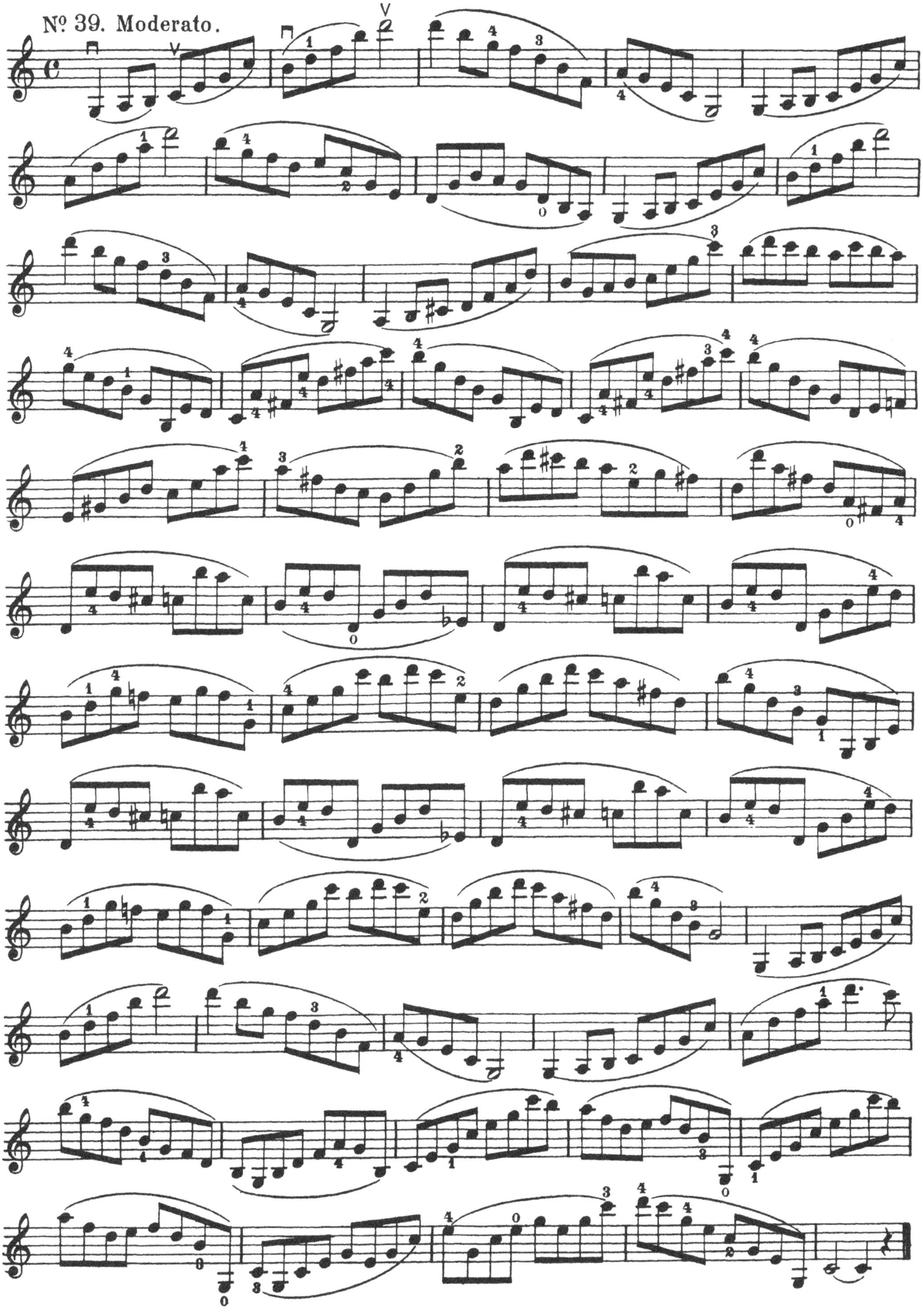

№ 40. **Allegro scherzando.** Springing bow (ricochet)

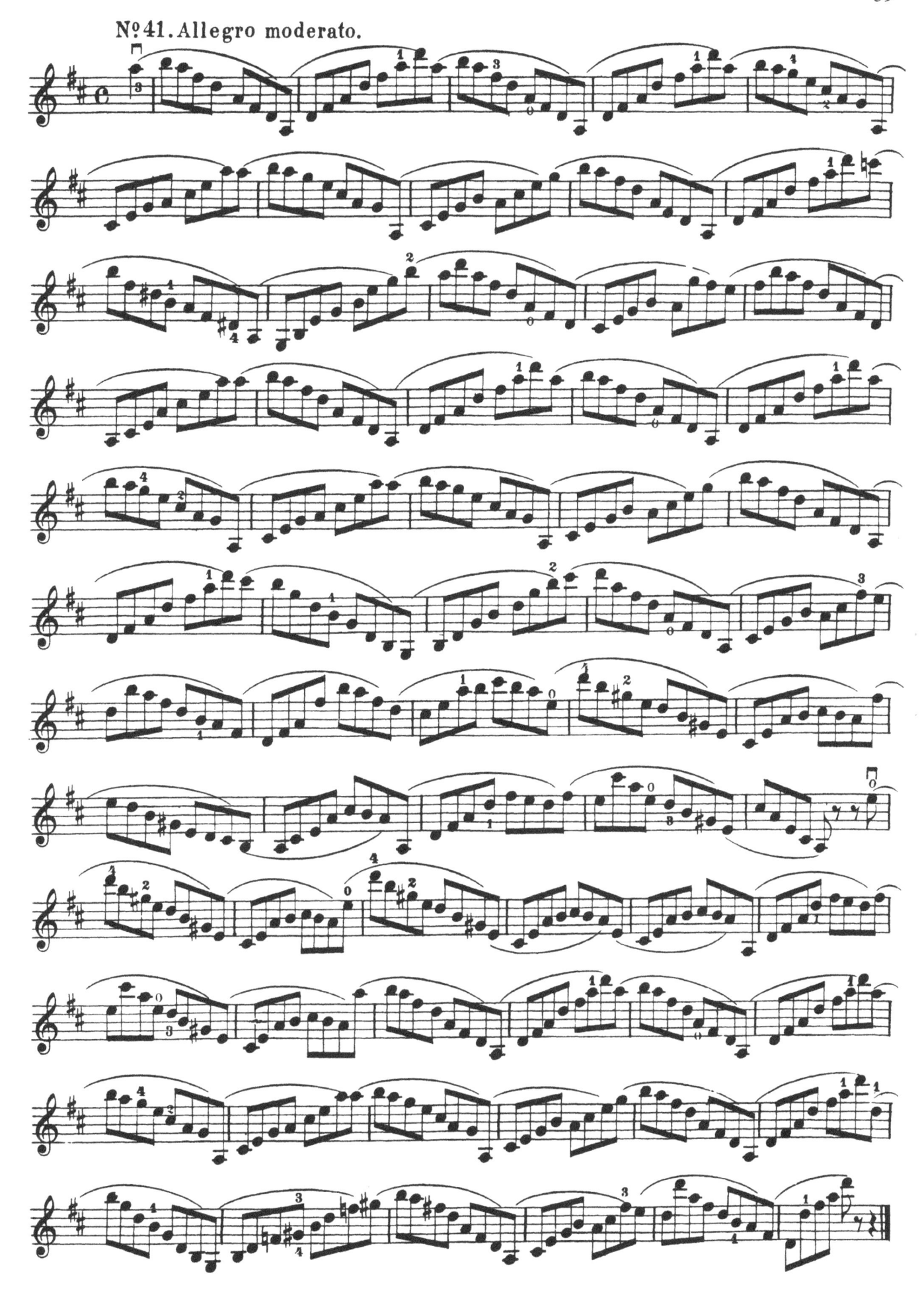

No 41. Allegro moderato.

№ 42. Andante.

№ 43. Moderato.

41

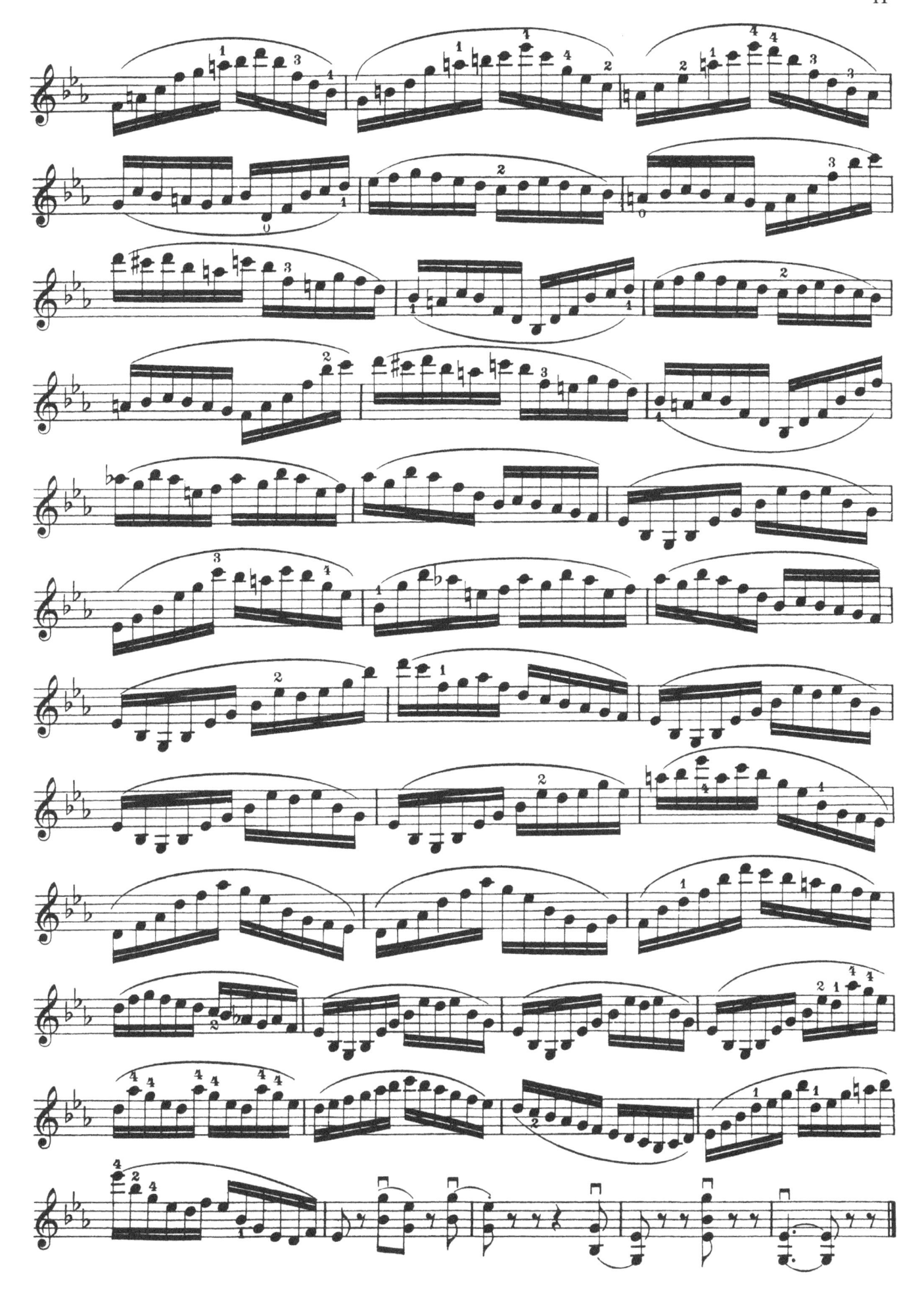

Nº 44. Tempo di marcia.

43

№46. Allegro.

No. 47. Andante cantabile.

No 48. Allegretto.

No 49. Allegro.

47

№ 50. Allegro.

No. 51. Moderato.

50

N.º 52. Andante.

N.º 53. Andante.

No 54. Allegro.

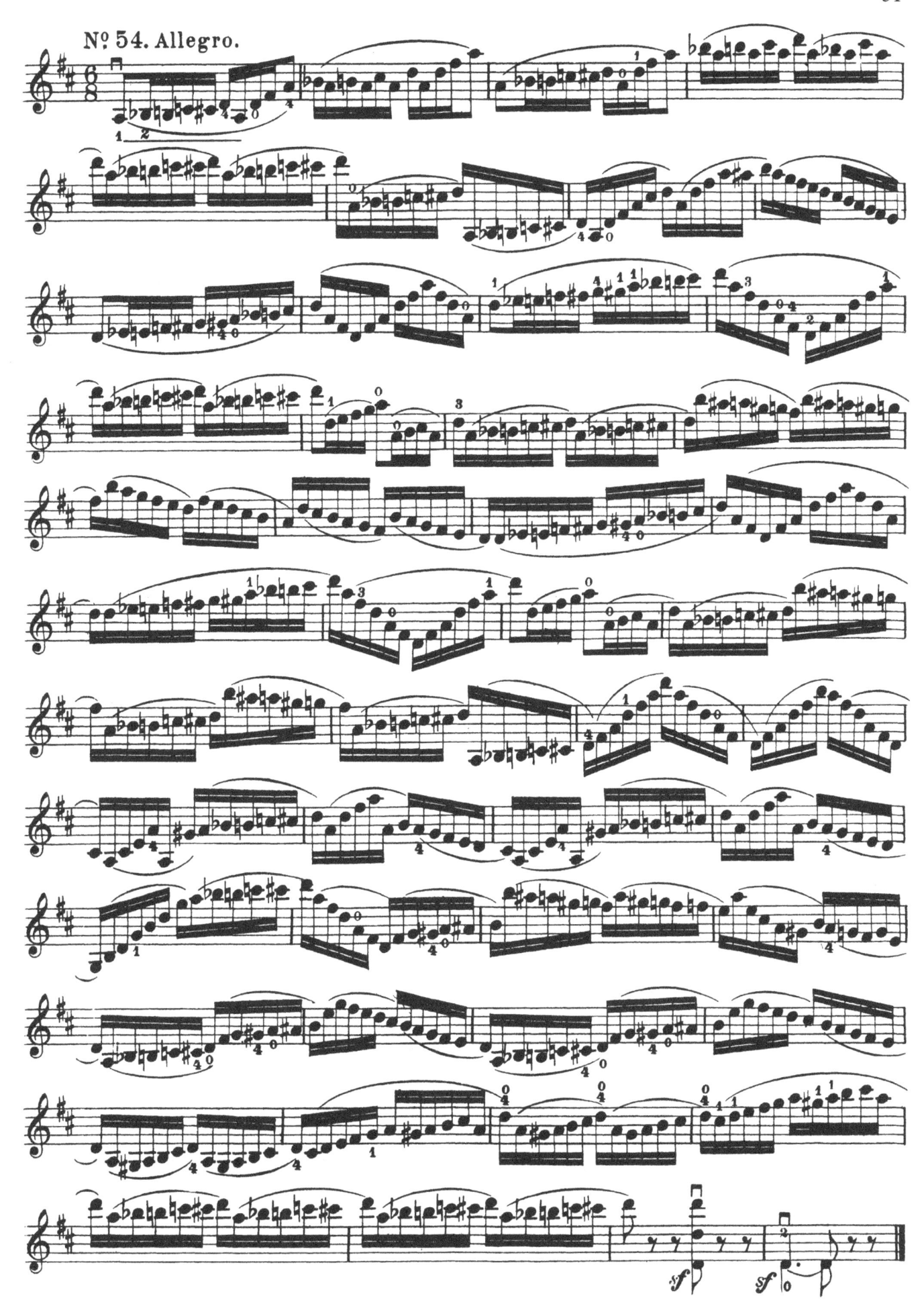

№ 55. Allegro.

№ 56. Andante.

Nº 57. Moderato assai.

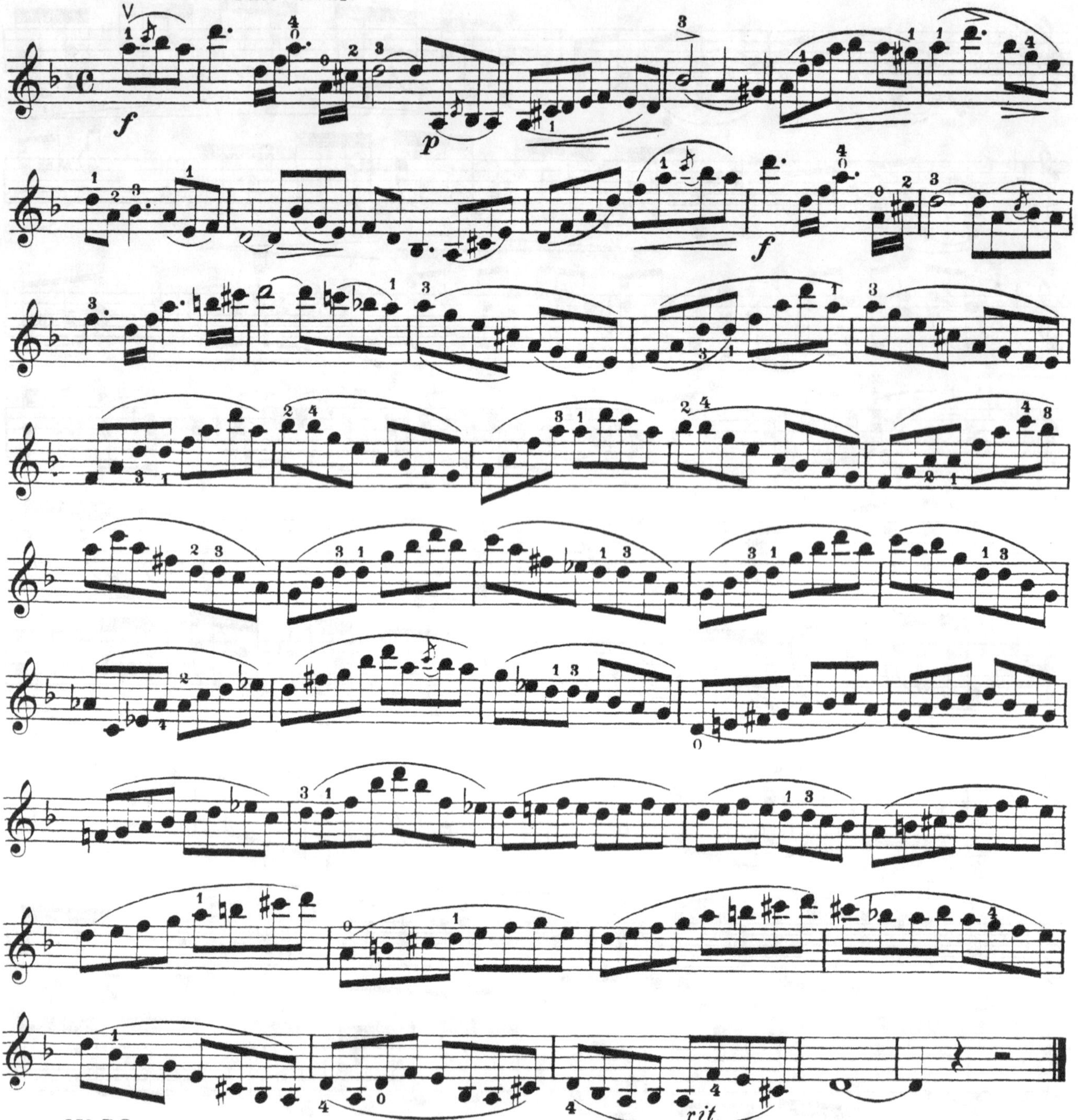

Nº 58. Andante.

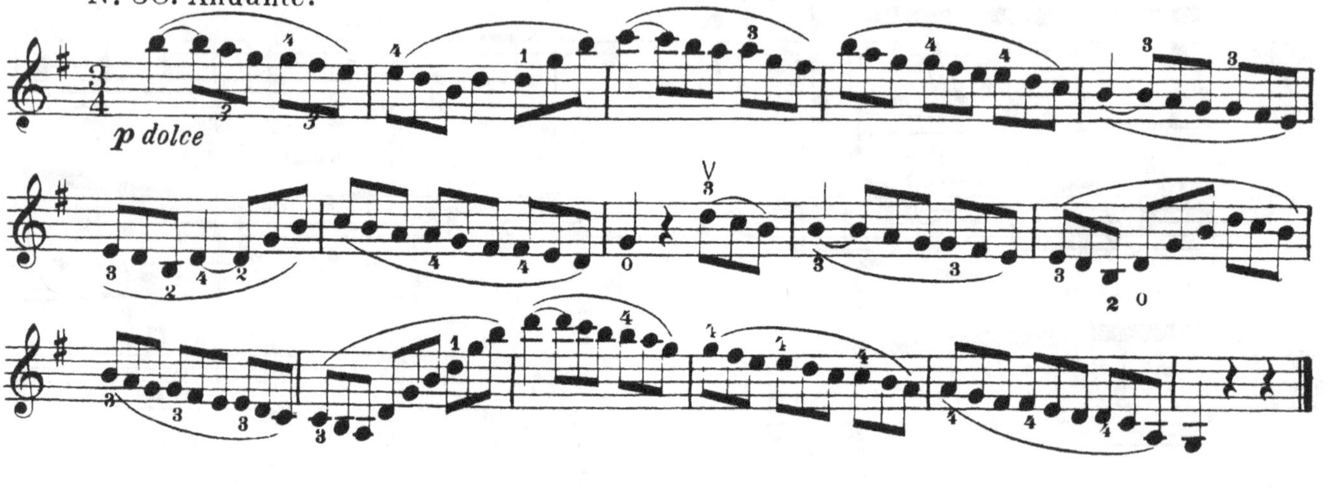

No 59. Moderato assai.

№ 60. Allegro con fuoco.

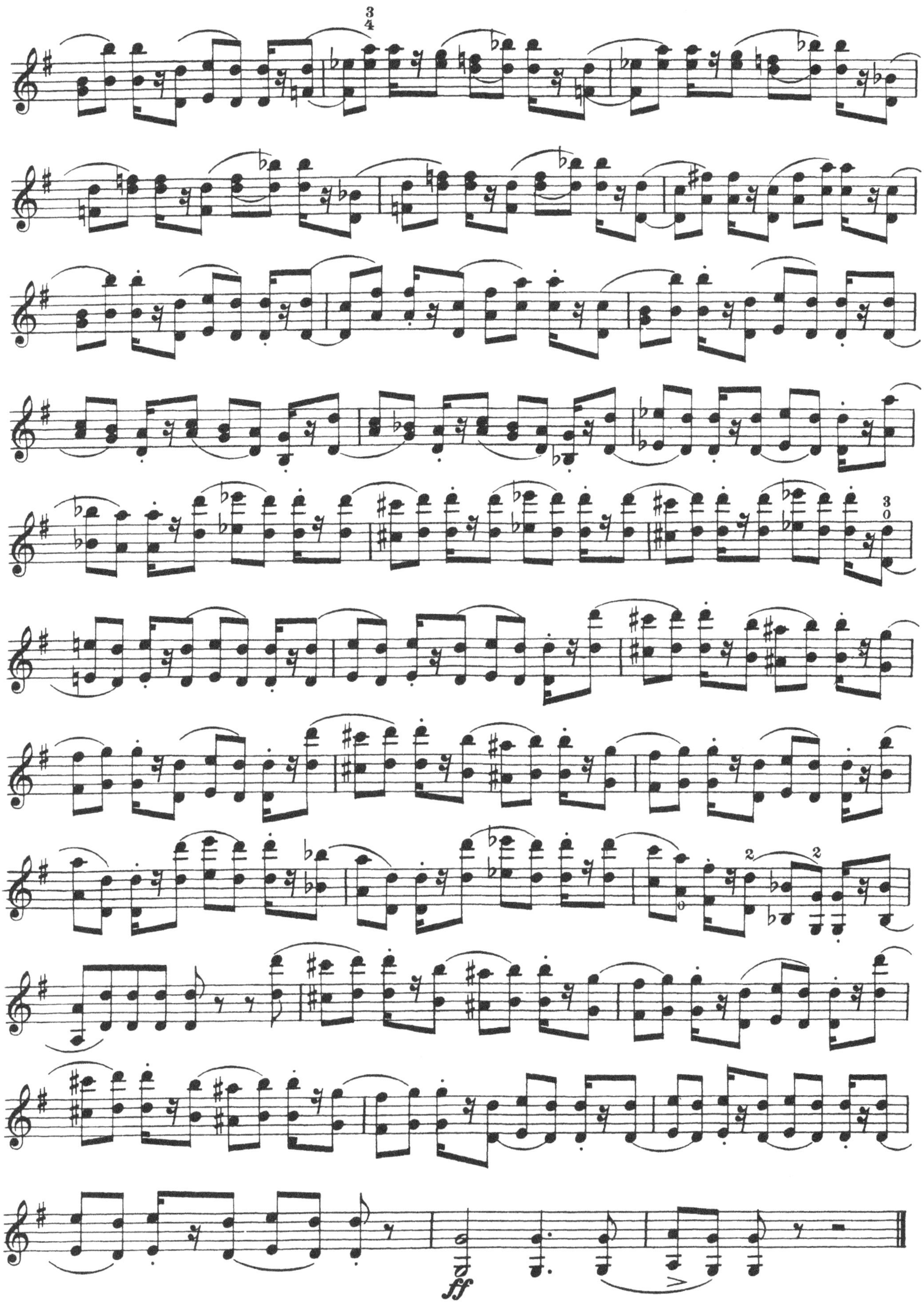
ff